REALITY
TV
TITANS

TASTEFUL FASHION WITH

Tim Gunn

WITHDRAWN

Jill C. Wheeler

**Checkerboard
Library**

An Imprint of Abdo Publishing
abdopublishing.com

abdopublishing.com

Published by Abdo Publishing, a division of ABDO, PO Box 398166, Minneapolis, Minnesota 55439. Copyright © 2016 by Abdo Consulting Group, Inc. International copyrights reserved in all countries. No part of this book may be reproduced in any form without written permission from the publisher. Checkerboard Library™ is a trademark and logo of Abdo Publishing.

Printed in the United States of America, North Mankato, Minnesota

062015

092015

Design: Jen Schoeller, Mighty Media, Inc.
Production: Christa Schneider, Mighty Media, Inc.
Series Editor: Liz Salzmann
Cover Photos: AP Images, front cover; Shutterstock, back cover
Interior Photos: AP Images, pp. 5, 9, 11, 15, 17, 21, 25, 27; Corbis, p. 23; iStockphoto, pp. 7, 13; Mighty Media, Inc., p. 19; Shutterstock, pp. 3, 20, 29

Library of Congress Cataloging-in-Publication Data

Wheeler, Jill C., 1964-
  Tasteful fashion with Tim Gunn / Jill C. Wheeler.
     pages cm. -- (Reality TV titans)
  Includes index.
  ISBN 978-1-62403-821-1
1. Gunn, Tim. 2. Fashion designers--United States--Biography--Juvenile literature. 3. Image consultants--United States--Biography--Juvenile literature. 4. Television personalities--United States--Biography--Juvenile literature. 5. Project runway (Television program)--Juvenile literature. 6. Fashion--New York (State)--New York--Juvenile literature. 7. Clothing and dress--New York (State)--New York--Juvenile literature. I. Title.
  TT505.G86W47 2015
  746.9'2092--dc23
  [B]

                              2015008102

CONTENTS

Tim Gunn

Tim Gunn is co-star of the reality television program *Project Runway*. It is a show where designers try to break into the fashion industry. Fashion is an industry filled with big egos. But Gunn is known as a kind, caring person. He is happy taking the **subway** instead of riding in a **limousine**. Model Heidi Klum worked with Gunn on *Project Runway*. She once called Gunn "the kindest, most humble person you have ever met."

Gunn's practical fashion advice has won him fans around the world. He has appeared on other television shows and movies. He is a frequent guest on talk shows. He also delivers public lectures on fashion issues.

Gunn survived a difficult childhood. He was a shy boy who was often bullied. He grew into one of America's best-loved television personalities. Today, Gunn helps young people overcome challenges and better understand who they are.

Fashion
guru
Tim Gunn

Washington Roots

Tim Gunn was born on July 29, 1953, in Washington, DC. His father, George, was an agent with the Federal Bureau of Investigation (FBI). His mother, Nancy, worked for the Central Intelligence Agency. Tim has a younger sister named Kim.

Gunn's father worked for FBI director J. Edgar Hoover. As a boy, Tim made several visits to FBI headquarters. However, Tim's quiet nature displeased his father. Though Gunn remembers his father as helpful, the two were never close.

Tim enjoyed designing and building **miniature** rooms. When Tim was nine, the family took a trip to Monticello, the home of Thomas Jefferson. Tim bought a book of Jefferson's **architectural** drawings. Back home, he built some of the rooms with Legos and his sister's Barbie toys.

DID YOU KNOW?
Tim studied piano for
12 years.

Tim's childhood visit to Monticello increased his interest in architecture.

Troubled Teen Years

In high school, Tim was a record-holding swimmer. Yet he never enjoyed sports that much. He also was uncomfortable in social situations. Part of his discomfort came from his having a stutter. Because of this, other students often bullied him.

Tim ran away from many different boarding schools because he was so miserable around the other children. He attended about 12 different schools between the ages of 12 and 20. When he was 17 years old, Tim attempted **suicide**. He swallowed a large number of pills. Luckily the attempt failed, and Tim woke up the next morning.

Tim spent the next two years in a special hospital. There, he worked with medical professionals to identify and treat the causes of his unhappiness. The professional help allowed him to turn his life around. However, because of the bad memories, Tim threw away nearly all of the pictures from his childhood.

As an adult, Tim would speak out against bullying for groups such as Peace Over Violence.

A Flair for Design

Gunn graduated from Woodrow Wilson High School in 1971. Following graduation, he studied English literature. At age 19, he took a drawing class. The class helped him realize he had special design talents. He understood then that his future was in design.

Gunn was particularly interested in sculpture. He went to the Corcoran School of Art in Washington, DC. In 1976, he graduated with a bachelor of fine arts degree in sculpture.

Gunn began his career building models for several **architectural** firms. He set up a studio to make the models out of paper and illustration board. He also worked as Corcoran's assistant director of **admissions**. That job included traveling around the United States to **recruit** students.

THE CORCORAN GALLERY OF ART

The Corcoran Gallery of Art and its associated school are today part of the National Gallery of Art.

Move to New York

In 1983, Gunn moved to New York, New York. He got a job at Parsons The New School for Design. Parsons is an art, fashion, and design school. Many famous designers attended Parsons. Gunn was Parson's assistant director of **admissions**. He talked to incoming students about their work.

Soon Gunn became a teacher at Parsons. He loved teaching! He thought that was odd since he had disliked being a student. The classes Gunn taught focused on **three-dimensional** design. He realized that sculpture was connected to fashion in that way.

Gunn worked his way up and became the school's associate **dean**. He created international programs for the school. He also developed ties between Parsons and design schools in France and Japan. Gunn had a calm, professional attitude. This made him the perfect person to talk with reporters about Parsons.

Parsons The New School for Design is in the David M. Schwartz Fashion Education Center building.

Making Changes

In 2000, Gunn became chair of Parson's Department of Fashion Design. When Gunn received the new assignment, the program had grown stale. Its students were poorly prepared for careers in the demanding, ever-changing fashion industry.

Gunn made it his mission to turn the fashion department around. He added a new program for senior-year students. It encouraged them to design their own garment collections. This helped the students learn more about their own abilities. The assignment also made them think about how their work fit with the larger design world.

Gunn worked with many successful fashion designers, sellers, and editors. They helped him reorganize the design program. Soon Parsons once again became a leader in fashion design education in the United States.

DID YOU KNOW?
When Gunn left Parsons, the school gave him the title of Honorary Chair of Fashion Design.

Gunn with fashion designers Tracy Reese, Kay Unger, and Carmen Marc Valvo at b the next. This event raises money for Parsons' Pre-College Scholars Program.

Parsons continues to be among the best of its kind in the world. What Gunn may not have realized is what his work for the school had done for his own reputation.

Project Runway

One day, Gunn received a phone call from the producers of a new television program. They called it *Project Runway*. On the show, designers would compete for a chance at a career in fashion. Because of his accomplishments at Parsons, the producers wanted Gunn to be a part of the project.

At first, Gunn was not interested. He told the producers he thought the idea sounded terrible. He thought a reality television show would only add to the fashion industry's problems. However, he agreed to meet with them. The producers eventually won Gunn over. He agreed to stage the first **episode** at Parsons. He also agreed to serve as **mentor** to the show's contestants for one year.

The season began with a group of designers who would compete against one another. Using special themes, they

DID YOU KNOW?
Cargo capri pants are Gunn's least favorite article of clothing.

were to create clothes with limited time and materials. Judges reviewed their designs. They eliminated one or more designers each week. At the end, only a few designers remained. Those designers would go on to compete in New York's Fashion Week.

Rising Star

The Bravo network showed the first **episode** of *Project Runway* in December 2004. Klum was its host. The show quickly became a hit. Gunn was supposed to advise the designers behind the scenes. Yet he quickly became as much of a star as Klum.

Gunn used honest criticism to challenge the contestants to improve their work. He focused on quality, taste, and style. He also helped mold the show. At first, the designers had other people to do the sewing. Gunn suggested that the designers should do their own sewing. He soon became known for his advice, "Make it work."

Gunn quickly became even more involved in the show. During the **audition** process, he reviewed the candidates' work in advance. He found himself stepping in when he saw a talented designer about to be eliminated. He sometimes asked the judges to let someone stay in spite of low scores. His plea to the judges became known as "Tim's Save." It became a feature on the show.

Inspired by Tim Gunn

Project Blazer

Materials
- **blazer or jacket**
- **non-permanent fabric marker or pencil**
- **a package of metal studs**

1. Ask an adult for help.

2. Lay the **blazer** on a flat surface.

3. Decide where you want to put the studs.

4. Draw your design on the blazer.

5. Following any directions on the packaging, add the studs according to your design.

Making It Work

Project Runway has been nominated for at least one **Emmy Award** every year. It won an Emmy for "Outstanding Host for a Reality or Reality-Competition Program" in 2013. Its popularity has also been credited for increased **enrollment** in design schools such as Parsons.

In 2007, Gunn left Parsons to become chief creative officer at Liz Claiborne. The fashion company had 350 designers. Gunn worked with them in a similar role to that on *Project Runway*. He listened to their ideas and offered suggestions and criticism to improve their projects.

Gunn also continued working with *Project Runway*. He became so popular he was a sought-after guest on other

Klum and Gunn with their Emmy Awards

shows. He appeared on *Drop Dead Diva*, *How I Met Your Mother*, and *Gossip Girl*, among others. In addition, he was a guest on talk shows and appeared in *The Smurfs* and other movies. Disney Junior asked Gunn to voice the character Baileywick on the television show *Sofia the First*. He also produced and hosted his own television show offering **makeovers** for women. *Tim Gunn's Guide to Style* ran from 2007 to 2008.

Beyond the Screen

In 2007, Gunn published his first book, *Tim Gunn: A Guide to Quality, Taste and Style*. He co-authored it with Kate Maloney. The two had worked together at Parsons. Gunn's next book came out in 2010. It's called *Gunn's Golden Rules: Life's Little Lessons for Making It Work*. This book is more personal and includes stories from Gunn's own life. In 2013 he published *Tim Gunn's Fashion Bible: The Fascinating History of Everything in Your Closet*.

Gunn has been a **mentor** to fashion and design students throughout his career. In 2015, he put some of those experiences in another book. It is titled *Tim Gunn: The Natty Professor*.

In 2014, Gunn launched the Tim Gunn Collection. It includes bedding and bath products sold on the QVC network. In designing the collection,

DID YOU KNOW?
Gunn loves to read. He has over 2,500 books in his apartment!

Gunn drew inspiration from the world of designer fashions. He looked at designing a bedroom the same way someone would put together an outfit. He also included some of his own favorite designs. Some designs in the collection were inspired by art he collected during his travels through Asia.

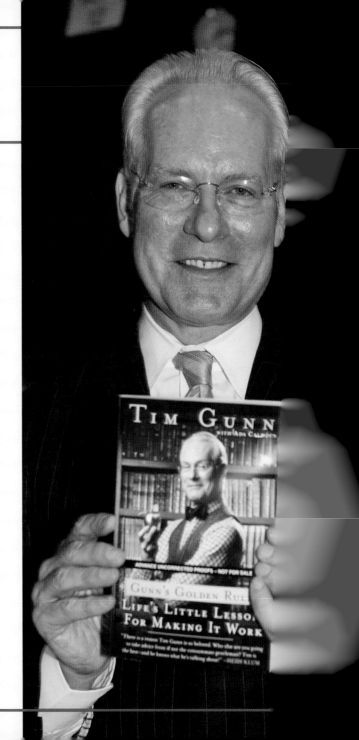

Giving Back

Gunn is involved with several charitable organizations. In 2010, he recorded a clip for the It Gets Better campaign. It Gets Better helps young people facing harassment for their sexuality.

This is a personal cause for Gunn. As a young man, he had been confused about his sexuality. He had faced harassment on an almost daily basis. It took many years for Gunn to accept himself for who he is.

Gunn is also active in the animal rights movement. He encourages the fashion industry to avoid using real fur. He also **narrated** a video for People For the Ethical Treatment of Animals (PETA). The video examined rabbit-fur farming practices.

Gunn hosted PETA's Fashion Week Bash in 2011. The event encouraged people to stop using animal fur.

New York Living

Today, Gunn still lives in New York City. He enjoys cooking and watching shows on the Home & Garden network. He visits New York's famed Metropolitan Museum of Art frequently. And few things make him happier than French fries!

Gunn hates driving. He often takes the **subway**. He doesn't mind that other riders ask him for **autographs** or fashion advice. But when Gunn's parents were alive, his mother often gave him fashion advice!

Gunn's father died before *Project Runway* began. His mother died in 2010. While she was alive, she was surprised at how famous her son had become. However, "She would be critical of what I would wear on the show," Gunn recalls. "In fact, she would call afterward and say, 'Why did they let you wear such-and-such? That tie didn't look good with that shirt!'" But Gunn's fans know he can always make it work!

DID YOU KNOW?
Gunn's favorite thing to cook is meatloaf. His secret ingredient is cheddar cheese!

A dapper Gunn in New York City

Timeline

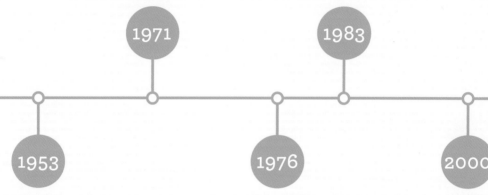

Gunn graduated from Woodrow Wilson High School.

Gunn moved to New York City and began working for Parsons The New School for Design.

1971

1983

1953

1976

2000

Tim Gunn was born on July 29th in Washington, DC.

Gunn graduated from the Corcoran School of Art.

Gunn became chair of Parson's Department of Fashion Design.

Tim Gunn Says

"The clothes we wear send a message about how the world perceives us."

"Life is not a solo act. It's a huge collaboration."

"I believe that treating other people well is a lost art."

The first episode of *Project Runway* aired on Bravo.

Gunn's book, *Gunn's Golden Rules: Life's Little Lessons For Making It Work*, was published.

Gunn launched the Tim Gunn Collection.

2004

2010

2014

2007

2013

Gunn started working for Liz Claiborne.

Project Runway won an Emmy Award.

"Take the high road. No matter how much stress, or strain, or consternation you are facing."

"I want to see greatness!"

"Make it work!"

Glossary

admissions – the department of a college responsible for attracting and accepting new students.

architectural – related to the design and construction of buildings.

audition – a short performance to test someone's ability.

autograph – a person's handwritten name.

blazer – a jacket that completes an outfit but is not part of a suit.

dean – a person at a college or university who is in charge of guiding students.

Emmy Award – one of several awards the Academy of Television Arts and Sciences presents to the year's best television programs, writers, and actors.

enrollment – the number of people registered, especially in order to attend a school.

episode – one show in a television series.

limousine – a large car driven by a professional driver.

makeover – a change of appearance, such as clothes, hairstyle, or makeup.

mentor – a trusted adviser or guide.

miniature – a copy of something in a reduced size.

narrate – to tell a story.

recruit – to get someone to join a group.

subway – an underground railroad.

suicide – the act of killing oneself.

three-dimensional – having three dimensions, such as length, width, and height. Something that is three-dimensional appears to have depth.

Websites

To learn more about Reality TV Titans, visit **booklinks.abdopublishing.com**. These links are routinely monitored and updated to provide the most current information available.

Index